Success Mindset for Entrepreneurs:
The Winning Habits and Mindset for Business Success

Dan M. Savage

Table of contents

- Vision, purpose and goal-setting
- Passion and Perseverance
- Risk-taking and decision making
- Resilience
- Creativity and innovation
- Adaptability and flexibility
- Networking and collaboration
- Time management
- Financial management and resource allocation
- Leadership and team-building
- Customer-centricity and marketing
- Continuous learning and personal growth

Chapter 1

Vision, purpose and goal-setting

Entrepreneurs are often described as visionaries because they have a clear idea of what they want to achieve and the impact they want to make. Having a vision, purpose, and goals are essential for entrepreneurs because they provide direction and focus. In this chapter, we will explore the importance of vision, purpose, and goal-setting for entrepreneurs and provide tips on how to develop and achieve them.

Defining Vision, Purpose, and Goals:

Vision: A vision is a clear and compelling description of what an entrepreneur wants to achieve in the long-term. It is the foundation for the business and serves as a roadmap for success. A vision should be ambitious, inspiring, and motivate entrepreneurs to take action.

Purpose: The purpose of a business is the reason why it exists beyond making a profit. It is the social or environmental impact that an entrepreneur wants to make through their business. Purpose-driven businesses often have a deeper sense of meaning and attract customers, employees, and investors who share the same values.

Goals: Goals are the specific objectives that an entrepreneur wants to achieve within a set timeframe. They should be measurable, realistic, and aligned with the vision and purpose of the business. Goals help entrepreneurs to stay on track, measure progress, and make adjustments as needed.

Developing a Vision, Purpose, and Goals:

- Identifying Values: An entrepreneur's values are the guiding principles that shape their decisions and actions. To develop a vision and purpose that align with their values, entrepreneurs need to identify what is important to them. They can do this by reflecting on their personal beliefs and experiences, observing the world around them, and seeking feedback from others.

- Creating a Vision: A vision should be based on an entrepreneur's values and aspirations for the future. To create a vision, entrepreneurs need to ask themselves questions such as "What do I want to achieve?" "What impact do I want to make?" and "What legacy do I want to leave?". They can also draw inspiration from their personal experiences, role models, and industry trends.

- Defining Purpose: An entrepreneur's purpose should be meaningful and aligned with their values and vision. To define their purpose, entrepreneurs need to ask themselves questions such as "What problem do I want to solve?" "What change do I want to make?" and "What difference do I want to create?". They can also seek input from stakeholders such as customers, employees, and partners.

- Setting Goals: Goals should be specific, measurable, achievable, relevant, and time-bound (SMART). To set goals, entrepreneurs need to break down their vision and purpose into smaller, actionable steps. They should also consider factors such as resources, timeline, and potential challenges.

Achieving Vision, Purpose, and Goals:

- Communicating Vision and Purpose: A vision and purpose are only effective if they are communicated clearly and consistently. Entrepreneurs should articulate their vision and purpose to stakeholders such as employees, customers, investors, and partners. They should also ensure that their actions and decisions are aligned with their vision and purpose.

- Monitoring Progress: Entrepreneurs should regularly monitor their progress towards their goals and make adjustments as needed. They can use metrics such as revenue, customer satisfaction, and employee engagement to track their performance. They should also celebrate milestones and recognize achievements.

- Embracing Flexibility: Entrepreneurship is a dynamic and

unpredictable journey, and entrepreneurs need to be flexible and adaptable to changes. They should be willing to pivot their vision, purpose, and goals based on feedback, market trends, and emerging opportunities.

Conclusion:

In conclusion, having a clear vision, purpose, and SMART goals are essential for entrepreneurs to succeed. Vision and purpose provide the direction and motivation that entrepreneurs need to achieve their goals, while SMART goals provide a clear roadmap to success. Entrepreneurs who take the time to develop a clear vision and purpose and set SMART goals are more likely to achieve their desired outcomes and create a positive impact on the world.

Summary:

- Entrepreneurs need a clear vision, purpose, and goals for direction and focus.
- Vision is a long-term description of what the entrepreneur wants to achieve.
- Purpose is the social or environmental impact beyond making a profit.
- Goals are measurable objectives that align with the vision and purpose.
- To develop vision, purpose, and goals, entrepreneurs need to identify their values and aspirations.
- Goals should be specific, measurable, achievable, relevant, and time-bound (SMART).
- Communicating the vision and purpose, monitoring progress, and embracing flexibility are crucial for achieving success.
- Having a clear vision, purpose, and SMART goals helps entrepreneurs create a positive impact on the world.

Chapter 2

Passion and Perseverance

As an entrepreneur, passion and perseverance are essential qualities to cultivate. Starting and growing a business can be a challenging and unpredictable journey, and it takes a deep-seated passion and unwavering perseverance to see through tough times and overcome obstacles. In this chapter, we'll explore the importance of passion and perseverance in entrepreneurship and provide some practical tips for cultivating these qualities.

Passion:

Passion is the fuel that drives entrepreneurs forward. It's the deep-seated love and commitment to the business idea and the desire to bring it to life. Without passion, it's difficult to stay motivated and committed to the long and often arduous journey of entrepreneurship.

To cultivate passion, start by:

- Identifying your "why": What drives you to pursue your business idea? What excites you about it? Identify the deeper meaning behind your business idea and focus on that to keep your passion alive.

- Staying connected to your customers: Your customers are the reason why you're in business. Stay connected to them and their needs to keep your passion for solving their problems alive.

- Surrounding yourself with like-minded people: Surround yourself with other entrepreneurs and individuals who share your passion and can provide support and encouragement when you need it.

Remember, passion is contagious. When you're passionate about your business, it's more likely that others will become passionate about it too, including customers, investors, and employees.

Perseverance:

Perseverance is the ability to keep going even when things get tough. It's the determination to overcome obstacles and setbacks, and to stay focused on the end goal.

To cultivate perseverance, start by:

- Embracing failure: Failure is a natural part of the entrepreneurial journey. Instead of fearing it, embrace it as an opportunity to learn and grow.

- Staying focused on the big picture: It's easy to get bogged down in the day-to-day challenges of running a business. Stay focused on the bigger picture and the long-term goal to keep your perseverance alive.

- Building a strong support system: Surround yourself with a network of supportive individuals who can provide guidance and encouragement when you need it.

Remember, perseverance is not about being stubborn or refusing to adapt to changing circumstances. It's about having the resilience to stay committed to your vision while being flexible and adaptable in your approach.

Conclusion:

In conclusion, passion and perseverance are critical qualities for entrepreneurial success.

Cultivate your passion by staying connected to your "why," your customers, and other like-minded individuals. Cultivate perseverance by embracing failure, staying focused on the big picture, and building a strong support system. Remember, passion and perseverance are not static qualities. They require ongoing cultivation and practice to stay alive and relevant throughout your entrepreneurial journey.

Summary:

- Passion and perseverance are essential qualities for entrepreneurs.
- Passion is the driving force that keeps entrepreneurs motivated and committed to their business idea.
- To cultivate passion, entrepreneurs should identify their "why," stay connected to their customers, and surround themselves with like-minded individuals.

- Perseverance is the ability to keep going even when faced with setbacks and obstacles.
- To cultivate perseverance, entrepreneurs should embrace failure, stay focused on the bigger picture, and build a strong support system.
- Passion and perseverance require ongoing cultivation and practice throughout the entrepreneurial journey.

Chapter 3

Risk-taking and decision making

Risk-taking and decision-making are two critical aspects of entrepreneurship. Starting and growing a business involves taking calculated risks and making bold decisions that can have significant impacts on the success or failure of the venture. In this chapter, we'll explore the importance of risk-taking and decision-making in entrepreneurship and provide some practical tips for cultivating these qualities.

Risk-Taking:

Entrepreneurship involves taking risks, but not all risks are created equal. Successful entrepreneurs take calculated risks that have the potential for high rewards. Here are some practical tips for cultivating the right mindset and approach to risk-taking:

- Be willing to fail: Failure is a natural part of the entrepreneurial journey. Embrace it as an opportunity to learn and grow, and don't be afraid to take risks that have the potential for failure.

- Do your research: Before taking a risk, do your due diligence. Research the market, competition, and potential outcomes of the risk you're considering. The more information you have, the better equipped you'll be to make informed decisions.

- Develop a contingency plan: Even the best-laid plans can go awry. Develop a contingency plan for potential outcomes and be prepared to pivot if necessary.

Remember, risk-taking is not about blindly jumping into unknown territory. It's about taking calculated risks that have the potential for high rewards while mitigating potential downsides.

Decision Making:

Entrepreneurship also involves making bold decisions that can have significant impacts on the success or failure of the venture. Here are some practical tips for cultivating the right mindset and approach to decision-making:

- Gather all available information: Before making a decision, gather as much information as possible. Research the market, competition, and potential outcomes of the decision you're considering.

- Consider the long-term impact: Think about the long-term impact of your decision. Will it help or hinder your progress towards your goals?

- Trust your instincts: While it's essential to gather information and consider the long-term impact of your decision, ultimately, you must trust your instincts and make the best decision for your business.

Remember, decision-making is not about making perfect decisions every time. It's about making informed decisions based on the available information and trusting your instincts.

Conclusion:

In conclusion, risk-taking and decision-making are critical qualities for entrepreneurial success. Cultivate a willingness to take calculated risks that have the potential for high rewards while mitigating potential downsides. Develop a mindset of gathering all available information, considering the long-term impact of your decisions, and trusting your instincts when making bold decisions. Remember, risk-taking and decision-making are not static qualities. They require ongoing cultivation and practice to stay alive and relevant throughout your entrepreneurial journey.

Summary:

Risk-taking:

- Entrepreneurship involves taking calculated risks that have the potential for high rewards.
- Embrace failure as an opportunity to learn and grow.
- Do your research before taking a risk and develop a contingency plan.
- Mitigate potential downsides of a risk.

Decision-making:

- Entrepreneurship also involves making bold decisions that can have significant impacts.
- Gather all available information and consider the long-term impact of your decision.
- Trust your instincts and make informed decisions based on available information.

Conclusion:

- Risk-taking and decision-making are critical qualities for entrepreneurial success.
- Cultivate a willingness to take calculated risks while mitigating potential downsides.
- Develop a mindset of gathering all available information, considering the long-term impact, and trusting your instincts when making bold decisions.

- These qualities require ongoing cultivation and practice throughout the entrepreneurial journey.

Chapter 4

Resilience

Entrepreneurship is not for the faint of heart. The journey to success is riddled with challenges, failures, and setbacks. To succeed as an entrepreneur, you must develop resilience—the ability to bounce back from failures and setbacks and keep moving forward. In this chapter, we'll explore the importance of resilience in entrepreneurship and provide practical tips for developing this critical quality.

What is Resilience?

Resilience is the ability to recover quickly from setbacks, adapt to change, and maintain a positive outlook despite difficult circumstances. It's not a fixed quality that you either have or don't have. Resilience is something that can be cultivated through intentional effort and practice.

The Importance of Resilience in Entrepreneurship:

Entrepreneurship is a roller coaster ride. One moment you're riding high on a wave of success, and the next, you're facing a major setback or failure. To succeed as an entrepreneur, you must develop resilience to bounce back from these challenges and keep moving forward. Here are some reasons why resilience is crucial for entrepreneurial success:

- Resilience helps you navigate uncertainty: The entrepreneurial journey is full of uncertainty. Resilience helps you stay calm and level-headed in the face of ambiguity and make informed decisions.

- Resilience helps you stay motivated: Entrepreneurship is a long and challenging journey. Resilience helps you stay motivated and focused on your goals, even in the face of setbacks and failures.

- Resilience helps you learn from failures: Failures and setbacks are inevitable in entrepreneurship. Resilience helps you learn from these experiences, adapt, and grow as an entrepreneur.

Tips for Developing Resilience:

Resilience is not something that comes naturally to everyone. It requires intentional effort and practice. Here are some practical tips for developing resilience:

- Cultivate a positive mindset: A positive outlook can help you bounce back from failures and setbacks. Focus on the things you're grateful for and try to find the silver lining in difficult situations.

- Build a support system: Surround yourself with people who believe in you and support your entrepreneurial journey. Having a network of friends, family, mentors, and colleagues can help you stay motivated and resilient.

- Practice self-care: Taking care of yourself physically, mentally, and emotionally is essential for developing resilience. Eat a healthy diet, get enough sleep, exercise regularly, and engage in activities that bring you joy and relaxation.

- Learn from failures: Every failure and setback is an opportunity to learn and grow as an entrepreneur. Take the time to reflect on what went wrong and what you can do differently next time.

Conclusion:

In conclusion, resilience is a critical quality for entrepreneurial success. It helps you navigate uncertainty, stay motivated, and learn from failures. Cultivate a positive mindset, build a support system, practice self-care, and learn from failures to develop resilience. Remember, resilience is not something that comes naturally to everyone. It requires intentional effort and practice. With the right mindset and approach, you can develop resilience and thrive as an entrepreneur.

Summary:

- Resilience is the ability to recover quickly from setbacks, adapt to change, and maintain a positive outlook despite difficult circumstances.

- Resilience is crucial for entrepreneurial success because it helps navigate uncertainty, stay motivated, and learn from failures.
- Resilience can be developed through intentional effort and practice.
- Tips for developing resilience include cultivating a positive mindset, building a support system, practicing self-care, and learning from failures.

Chapter 5

Creativity and innovation

Creativity and innovation are critical qualities for entrepreneurs who want to succeed in a crowded marketplace. To stand out from the competition, entrepreneurs must be able to generate unique and innovative ideas. In this chapter, we'll explore the importance of creativity and innovation in entrepreneurship and provide some practical tips for cultivating these qualities.

Understanding Creativity and Innovation:

Creativity is the ability to generate new and unique ideas. Innovation, on the other hand, is the process of taking those ideas and turning them into something valuable.

Creativity and innovation are closely linked and essential for entrepreneurial success.

Cultivating Creativity:

Here are some practical tips for cultivating creativity in entrepreneurship:

- Practice brainstorming: Brainstorming is a technique that involves generating a large number of ideas in a short period of time. This technique can help you generate a wide range of ideas and stimulate your creativity.

- Take breaks: Taking breaks and allowing your mind to wander can help stimulate creativity. Take breaks throughout the day to go for a walk, meditate, or engage in other activities that help you relax and clear your mind.

- Surround yourself with inspiration: Surround yourself with things that inspire you. This could include artwork, music, or books. Immersing yourself in creativity can help you generate new ideas and stimulate your imagination.

- Experiment: Experiment with new approaches and ideas. Don't be afraid to try something new, even if it seems unconventional. This can help you generate new and unique ideas.

Generating Innovative Ideas:

Here are some practical tips for generating innovative ideas in entrepreneurship:

- Look for gaps in the market: Identify gaps in the market that you can fill with a unique product or service. This could involve identifying an unmet need or finding a way to improve upon an existing product or service.

- Ask for feedback: Ask for feedback from customers and other stakeholders. This can help you identify areas for improvement and generate new ideas.

- Collaborate with others: Collaborating with others can help you generate new ideas and approaches. Working with people from diverse backgrounds and skillsets can help you come up with innovative solutions to problems.

- Stay informed: Stay up-to-date with industry trends and developments. This can help you identify new opportunities and generate innovative ideas.

Remember, creativity and innovation are skills that can be developed and improved over time. By cultivating your creativity and learning to generate innovative ideas, you can set yourself apart in a crowded marketplace and increase your chances of entrepreneurial success.

Conclusion:

In conclusion, creativity and innovation are critical qualities for entrepreneurial success. To cultivate creativity, practice brainstorming, take breaks, surround yourself with inspiration, and experiment with new approaches. To generate innovative ideas, look for gaps in the market, ask for feedback, collaborate with others, and stay informed. Remember, creativity and innovation are skills that can be developed and improved over time. By consistently working to cultivate these qualities, you can increase your chances of entrepreneurial success.

Summary:

- Creativity and innovation are critical for entrepreneurial success in a crowded marketplace.
- Creativity is the ability to generate new and unique ideas, while innovation is the process of turning those ideas into something valuable.
- Practical tips for cultivating creativity in entrepreneurship include brainstorming, taking breaks, surrounding yourself with inspiration, and experimenting with new approaches.
- Practical tips for generating innovative ideas in entrepreneurship include looking for gaps in the market, asking for feedback, collaborating with others, and staying informed of industry trends and developments.
- Remember, creativity and innovation can be developed and improved over time.

Chapter 6

Adaptability and flexibility

In today's rapidly changing business environment, entrepreneurs must be adaptable and flexible. Market conditions and customer needs can change quickly, and entrepreneurs who can respond and pivot effectively are more likely to succeed. In this chapter, we'll explore the importance of adaptability and flexibility in entrepreneurship and provide some practical strategies for staying nimble in the face of change.

The Importance of Adaptability and Flexibility:

Adaptability and flexibility are critical qualities for entrepreneurs to possess. Here's why:

- Responding to market changes: Market conditions can change quickly, and entrepreneurs who are able to pivot and adapt to new circumstances are more likely to succeed.

- Meeting customer needs: Customer needs can change over time, and entrepreneurs who are able to respond to those changes by adjusting their products or services are more likely to retain customers and attract new ones.

- Staying ahead of the competition: In a crowded marketplace, entrepreneurs who can innovate and adapt to new trends and technologies are more likely to stand out from the competition.

Strategies for Staying Adaptable and Flexible:

Here are some practical strategies for staying adaptable and flexible in entrepreneurship:

- Be open-minded: Be open to new ideas and perspectives. Don't get stuck in a rigid mindset or approach.

- Embrace change: Rather than resisting change, embrace it. Look for opportunities to innovate and improve.

- Stay informed: Keep up with industry trends and changes in the marketplace. Stay on top of what your competitors are doing.

- Pivot when necessary: Don't be afraid to pivot your business strategy when necessary. Be willing to change course if it's in the best interest of your business.

- Test and iterate: Test new ideas and products and be willing to iterate and make changes based on feedback.

- Build a strong team: Build a team that is adaptable and flexible. Hire people who are open-minded and can pivot when necessary.

Overcoming Challenges to Adaptability and Flexibility:

There are some common challenges that can hinder adaptability and flexibility in entrepreneurship. Here's how to overcome them:

- Fear of failure: Fear of failure can prevent entrepreneurs from taking risks and trying new things. Embrace failure as a learning opportunity and use it to inform your next steps.

- Resistance to change: Resistance to change can stem from a desire to maintain the status quo or a lack of understanding of the benefits of change. Communicate the benefits of change to your team and be willing to lead by example.

- Lack of resources: Limited resources can make it challenging to pivot or innovate. Look for creative solutions and don't be afraid to reach out for help or collaborate with others.

Conclusion:

In conclusion, adaptability and flexibility are critical qualities for entrepreneurial success. Stay open-minded, embrace change, stay informed, pivot when necessary, test and iterate, and build a strong team. Overcome challenges to adaptability and flexibility by embracing failure, communicating the benefits of change, and looking for creative solutions. Remember, adaptability and flexibility are skills that can be developed and improved over time. With practice and persistence, you can become a more adaptable and flexible entrepreneur.

Summary:

- Adaptability and flexibility are essential qualities for entrepreneurial success due to the rapidly changing business environment.
- Entrepreneurs who are adaptable and flexible are better able to respond to market changes, meet customer needs, and stay ahead of the competition.
- Strategies for staying adaptable and flexible include being open-minded, embracing change, staying informed, pivoting when necessary, testing and iterating, and building a strong team.
- Common challenges to adaptability and flexibility include fear of failure,

resistance to change, and lack of
resources.

- Overcoming these challenges involves
  embracing failure, communicating the
  benefits of change, and looking for
  creative solutions.
- Adaptability and flexibility are skills
  that can be developed and improved
  over time with practice and
  persistence.

Chapter 7

Networking and collaboration

Networking and collaboration are essential components of entrepreneurship. In order to build a successful business, entrepreneurs need to build a strong network of contacts and collaborators who can help them achieve their goals. In this chapter, we'll explore the importance of networking and collaboration in entrepreneurship and provide some practical strategies for building a strong network and leveraging relationships to drive growth.

Understanding Networking and Collaboration:

Networking involves building and maintaining relationships with people who can provide support, advice, and access to resources. Collaboration involves working with others to achieve common goals. Networking and collaboration go hand in hand, as entrepreneurs often collaborate with their network to achieve their goals.

Building a Strong Network:

Here are some practical strategies for building a strong network in entrepreneurship:

- Attend networking events: Attend networking events in your industry or community to meet new people and expand your network.

- Join industry associations: Join industry associations or groups to connect with other professionals in your field.

- Use social media: Use social media platforms like LinkedIn and Twitter to connect with other entrepreneurs and industry leaders.

- Offer value: Offer value to others by sharing your expertise, resources, or connections.

- Follow up: Follow up with new contacts after networking events or meetings to maintain the relationship.

Leveraging Relationships:

Here are some practical strategies for leveraging relationships in entrepreneurship:

- Collaborate on projects: Collaborate with other entrepreneurs or businesses on projects to achieve common goals.

- Ask for referrals: Ask your network for referrals or introductions to potential clients or customers.

- Seek advice: Seek advice and guidance from mentors or trusted advisors in your network.

- Offer opportunities: Offer opportunities to others in your network, such as speaking engagements or guest blog posts.

- Show appreciation: Show appreciation to your network by thanking them for their support and contributions.

Building a Culture of Collaboration:

Here are some additional strategies for building a culture of collaboration within your business:

- Foster open communication: Foster open communication and encourage team members to share ideas and feedback.

- Embrace diversity: Embrace diversity in your team and encourage collaboration among people with different backgrounds and perspectives.

- Encourage cross-functional teams: Encourage cross-functional teams to work together on projects to promote collaboration across departments.

- Provide incentives: Provide incentives or rewards for collaboration, such as bonuses or recognition programs.

- Lead by example: Lead by example by collaborating with others and demonstrating the value of teamwork.

Conclusion:

In conclusion, networking and collaboration are essential components of entrepreneurship. Build a strong network by attending networking events, joining industry associations, using social media, offering value, and following up. Leverage relationships by collaborating on projects, asking for referrals, seeking advice, offering opportunities, and showing appreciation. Build a culture of collaboration within your business by fostering open communication, embracing diversity, encouraging cross-functional teams, providing incentives, and leading by example. Remember, networking and collaboration are skills that can be developed and improved over time. With practice and persistence, you can become a more effective networker and collaborator.

Summary:

Importance of Networking and Collaboration:

- Networking and collaboration are essential components of entrepreneurship.
- Networking involves building and maintaining relationships, while collaboration involves working with others to achieve common goals.
- Entrepreneurs often collaborate with their network to achieve their goals.

Building a Strong Network:

- Attend networking events, join industry associations, use social media, offer value, and follow up with new contacts.

Leveraging Relationships:

- Collaborate on projects, ask for referrals, seek advice, offer opportunities, and show appreciation to your network.

Building a Culture of Collaboration:

- Foster open communication, embrace diversity, encourage cross-functional teams, provide incentives, and lead by example.

Conclusion:

- Networking and collaboration are skills that can be developed and improved over time.
- With practice and persistence, entrepreneurs can become more effective networkers and collaborators.

Chapter 8

Time management

Time management is a critical skill for entrepreneurs who are often juggling multiple responsibilities. In this chapter, we'll explore the importance of time management in entrepreneurship and provide practical strategies for prioritizing tasks and managing time effectively.

The Importance of Time Management:

Effective time management is essential for entrepreneurs for several reasons:

- Maximize productivity: When you manage your time effectively, you can maximize your productivity and get more done in less time.

- Reduce stress: When you have a clear plan for how to use your time, you can reduce stress and anxiety related to feeling overwhelmed or uncertain about what to do next.

- Achieve goals: When you prioritize tasks and manage your time effectively, you can achieve your goals more efficiently and effectively.

Prioritizing Tasks:

One of the most important aspects of time management is prioritizing tasks. Here are some practical strategies for prioritizing tasks:

- Make a to-do list: Start each day by making a to-do list of tasks that need to be completed.

- Use the 80/20 rule: Focus on the 20% of tasks that will generate 80% of the results.

- Identify urgent and important tasks: Prioritize tasks based on urgency and importance.

- Delegate tasks: Delegate tasks that can be done by others to free up your time for higher-priority tasks.

Managing Time Effectively:

In addition to prioritizing tasks, managing time effectively is crucial for entrepreneurs. Here are some practical strategies for managing time effectively:

- Set realistic deadlines: Set realistic deadlines for tasks to avoid overloading your schedule.

- Use time-blocking: Block off chunks of time on your calendar for specific tasks to help you stay focused and avoid distractions.

- Avoid multitasking: Focus on one task at a time to avoid distractions and improve productivity.

- Take breaks: Take regular breaks to avoid burnout and stay fresh and focused.

Using Tools and Technology:

There are many tools and technologies available to help entrepreneurs manage their time effectively. Here are some examples:

- Time-tracking apps: Use time-tracking apps like Toggl or RescueTime to monitor how you spend your time and identify areas for improvement.

- Productivity apps: Use productivity apps like Asana or Trello to manage tasks and collaborate with others.

- Calendar apps: Use calendar apps like Google Calendar or Outlook to schedule tasks and appointments and avoid overbooking your schedule.

- Automation tools: Use automation tools like Zapier or IFTTT to automate repetitive tasks and save time.

Conclusion:

In conclusion, time management is a critical skill for entrepreneurs who are often juggling multiple responsibilities. Prioritize tasks by making a to-do list, using the 80/20 rule, identifying urgent and important tasks, and delegating tasks. Manage time effectively by setting realistic deadlines, using time-blocking, avoiding multitasking, and taking breaks. Use tools and technologies like time-tracking apps, productivity apps, calendar apps, and automation tools to streamline tasks and save time. Remember, effective time management is a skill that can be developed and improved over time. With practice and persistence, you can prioritize tasks and manage time effectively to achieve your goals and maximize productivity in your business.

Summary:

- Effective time management is critical for entrepreneurs who juggle multiple responsibilities.
- Prioritizing tasks maximizes productivity, reduces stress, and helps achieve goals.
- Strategies for prioritizing tasks include making a to-do list, using the 80/20 rule, identifying urgent and important tasks, and delegating tasks.

- Managing time effectively includes setting realistic deadlines, using time-blocking, avoiding multitasking, and taking breaks.
- Tools and technologies like time-tracking apps, productivity apps, calendar apps, and automation tools can help streamline tasks and save time.
- Effective time management is a skill that can be developed and improved over time with practice and persistence.

Chapter 9

Financial management and resource allocation

Financial management and resource allocation are essential skills for entrepreneurs who want to build successful and sustainable businesses. In this chapter, we'll explore the importance of financial management in entrepreneurship and provide some practical strategies for managing cash flow, securing funding, and making smart financial decisions.

Understanding Financial Management:

Financial management is the process of planning, organizing, and controlling how you use your financial resources. It's about making the most of the money you have by creating and sticking to a budget, managing cash flow, and making informed financial decisions. Effective financial management can help you avoid financial problems, maximize profits, and ensure the long-term sustainability of your business.

Managing Cash Flow:

Cash flow is the amount of money that comes in and goes out of your business over a period of time. It's important to manage cash flow effectively to ensure that you have enough money to cover expenses and invest in growth opportunities. Here are some strategies for managing cash flow:

- Create a cash flow forecast: Create a cash flow forecast to predict your future cash inflows and outflows.

- Monitor your cash flow regularly: Monitor your cash flow regularly to identify potential issues and opportunities.

- Keep a cash reserve: Keep a cash reserve to cover unexpected expenses or emergencies.

- Negotiate payment terms: Negotiate payment terms with suppliers and customers to improve cash flow.

Securing Funding:

Securing funding is often a critical part of starting and growing a business. Here are some strategies for securing funding:

- Bootstrapping: Bootstrapping involves funding your business with your own resources, such as personal savings or credit cards.

- Crowdfunding: Crowdfunding involves raising money from a large number of people through platforms like Kickstarter or Indiegogo.

- Angel investors: Angel investors are individuals who invest their own money in early-stage startups in exchange for equity.

- Venture capital: Venture capital involves raising money from professional investors who provide funding in exchange for equity.

Making Smart Financial Decisions:

Making smart financial decisions is crucial for building a successful business. Here are some strategies for making smart financial decisions:

- Create a budget: Create a budget to plan and track your income and expenses.

- Evaluate opportunities: Evaluate opportunities based on their potential return on investment (ROI).

- Analyze financial statements: Analyze financial statements like income statements and balance sheets to make informed financial decisions.

- Seek expert advice: Seek expert advice from accountants or financial advisors to make informed financial decisions.

Conclusion:

In conclusion, financial management and resource allocation are essential skills for entrepreneurs who want to build successful and sustainable businesses. Manage cash flow by creating a cash flow forecast, monitoring cash flow regularly, keeping a cash reserve, and negotiating payment terms. Secure funding by bootstrapping, crowdfunding, seeking angel investors, or venture capital. Make smart financial decisions by creating a budget, evaluating opportunities, analyzing financial statements, and seeking expert advice. Remember, financial management is a skill that can be developed and improved over time. With practice and persistence, you can manage your finances effectively and build a successful business.

Summary:

- Financial management is crucial for entrepreneurs to build successful and sustainable businesses.
- Financial management involves planning, organizing, and controlling the use of financial resources.
- Effective financial management can help avoid financial problems, maximize profits, and ensure long-term sustainability.

- Cash flow management is important for covering expenses and investing in growth opportunities.
- Strategies for managing cash flow include creating a forecast, monitoring regularly, keeping a cash reserve, and negotiating payment terms.
- Funding can be secured through bootstrapping, crowdfunding, angel investors, or venture capital.
- Smart financial decisions involve creating a budget, evaluating opportunities based on ROI, analyzing financial statements, and seeking expert advice.
- Financial management is a skill that can be developed and improved over time.

Chapter 10

Leadership and team-building

Leadership and team-building are essential skills for entrepreneurs who want to build successful and sustainable businesses. In this chapter, we'll explore the importance of leadership and team-building in entrepreneurship and provide some practical strategies for developing strong leadership skills and building a high-performing team.

Understanding Leadership:

Leadership is the ability to inspire and motivate others to achieve a common goal. Effective leadership involves setting a clear vision, communicating that vision to your team, and providing guidance and support to help them achieve their goals. Here are some strategies for developing strong leadership skills:

- Set a clear vision: Set a clear vision for your business that inspires and motivates your team.

- Lead by example: Lead by example by demonstrating the behaviors and values you want to see in your team.

- Communicate effectively: Communicate effectively with your team to ensure everyone understands the vision and their role in achieving it.

- Provide guidance and support: Provide guidance and support to your team to help them achieve their goals.

Building a High-Performing Team:

Building a high-performing team is essential for achieving your business goals. Here are some strategies for building a high-performing team:

- Hire the right people: Hire the right people who share your vision and values and have the skills and experience to help you achieve your goals.

- Create a positive work environment: Create a positive work environment that fosters collaboration, creativity, and innovation.

- Develop a strong culture: Develop a strong culture that promotes teamwork, accountability, and continuous improvement.

- Provide opportunities for growth and development: Provide opportunities for growth and development to help your team members reach their full potential.

Motivating Your Team:

Motivating your team is essential for achieving your business goals. Here are some strategies for motivating your team:

- Recognize and reward achievement: Recognize and reward achievement to encourage your team members to work hard and achieve their goals.

- Provide feedback: Provide feedback to help your team members improve and grow.

- Set goals and track progress: Set goals and track progress to help your team members stay focused and motivated.

- Lead by example: Lead by example by demonstrating the behaviors and values you want to see in your team.

Conclusion:

In conclusion, leadership and team-building are essential skills for entrepreneurs who want to build successful and sustainable businesses. Develop strong leadership skills by setting a clear vision, leading by example, communicating effectively, and providing guidance and support. Build a high-performing team by hiring the right people, creating a positive work environment, developing a strong culture, and providing opportunities for growth and development. Motivate your team by recognizing and rewarding achievement, providing feedback, setting goals and tracking progress, and leading by example. Remember, leadership and team-building are skills that can be developed and improved over time. With practice and persistence, you can become an effective leader and build a high-performing team.

Summary:

- Leadership and team-building are essential skills for entrepreneurs.
- Effective leadership involves setting a clear vision, leading by example, communicating effectively, and providing guidance and support.
- Building a high-performing team involves hiring the right people, creating a positive work environment, developing a strong culture, and providing growth opportunities.
- Motivating your team involves recognizing and rewarding achievement, providing feedback, setting goals and tracking progress, and leading by example.
- These skills can be developed and improved over time with practice and persistence.

Chapter 11

Customer-centricity and marketing

Customer-centricity and marketing are essential components of building a successful and sustainable business. Understanding the needs and preferences of your customers is crucial for developing products and services that meet their needs, building brand loyalty, and driving growth. In this chapter, we will explore the importance of customer-centricity and marketing in entrepreneurship and provide practical strategies for staying customer-focused and delivering value to customers.

Understanding Customer-Centricity:

Customer-centricity is the philosophy of putting the customer at the center of your business. It involves understanding the needs and preferences of your customers and using that knowledge to inform your product development, marketing, and customer service strategies. Here are some strategies for developing a customer-centric mindset:

- Conduct market research: Conduct market research to gain insights into your customers' needs, preferences, and behaviors.

- Develop customer personas: Develop customer personas to better understand the demographics, psychographics, and pain points of your target audience.

- Use customer feedback: Use customer feedback to continually improve your products and services and better meet the needs of your customers.

- Create a customer-focused culture: Create a culture that prioritizes the needs of your customers and empowers employees to deliver exceptional customer service.

Creating a Marketing Strategy:

Marketing is the process of promoting your products or services to your target audience. A successful marketing strategy should be customer-focused and designed to meet the needs and preferences of your customers. Here are some strategies for developing an effective marketing strategy:

- Identify your target audience: Identify your target audience and develop customer personas to better understand their needs and preferences.

- Develop a unique value proposition: Develop a unique value proposition that differentiates your products or services from those of your competitors.

- Choose the right marketing channels: Choose the right marketing channels to reach your target audience, whether that be social media, email marketing, or traditional advertising.

- Measure your results: Measure your marketing results and use that data to continually improve your marketing strategy.

Providing Exceptional Customer Service:

Providing exceptional customer service is essential for building customer loyalty and driving growth. Here are some strategies for providing exceptional customer service:

- Train your employees: Train your employees to provide exceptional customer service and empower them to make decisions that prioritize the needs of your customers.

- Respond quickly: Respond quickly to customer inquiries and complaints to show that you value their business.

- Personalize the experience: Personalize the customer experience by using customer data to provide tailored recommendations and offers.

- Continuously improve: Continuously improve your customer service strategy by collecting and analyzing customer feedback.

Conclusion:

In conclusion, customer-centricity and marketing are essential components of building a successful and sustainable business. Develop a customer-centric mindset by conducting market research, developing customer personas, using customer feedback, and creating a customer-focused culture. Develop an effective marketing strategy by identifying your target audience, developing a unique value proposition, choosing the right marketing channels, and measuring your results. Provide exceptional customer service by training your employees, responding quickly, personalizing the experience, and continuously improving your strategy. Remember, customer-centricity and marketing are ongoing processes that require continuous improvement and adaptation to stay relevant and effective. With a customer-focused mindset and a well-executed marketing strategy, you can build a loyal customer base and drive sustainable growth for your business.

Summary:

- Customer-centricity and marketing are crucial for building a successful and sustainable business.
- Customer-centricity involves putting the customer at the center of your business and understanding their needs and preferences.
- Strategies for developing a customer-centric mindset include conducting market research, developing customer personas, using customer feedback, and creating a customer-focused culture.
- Marketing is the process of promoting your products or services to your target audience, and an effective marketing strategy should be customer-focused.

- Strategies for developing an effective marketing strategy include identifying your target audience, developing a unique value proposition, choosing the right marketing channels, and measuring your results.
- Providing exceptional customer service is essential for building customer loyalty and driving growth.
- Strategies for providing exceptional customer service include training your employees, responding quickly, personalizing the experience, and continuously improving your strategy.
- Customer-centricity and marketing are ongoing processes that require continuous improvement and adaptation to stay relevant and effective.

Chapter 12

Continuous learning and personal growth

Entrepreneurship is a journey that requires continuous learning and personal growth. In order to succeed, entrepreneurs need to be adaptable, curious, and willing to embrace new ideas and perspectives. This chapter explores the importance of continuous learning and personal growth in entrepreneurship, and provides insights on how to cultivate a mindset of lifelong learning.

Why Continuous Learning and Personal Growth are Essential for Entrepreneurs?

The world of business is constantly changing, and entrepreneurs need to keep up with these changes in order to remain relevant and competitive. Continuous learning and personal growth are essential for entrepreneurs for several reasons:

- Adapting to Changing Market Conditions: In order to succeed, entrepreneurs need to be able to adapt to changing market conditions. This requires a willingness to learn about new technologies, customer needs, and emerging trends.

- Improving Skills and Knowledge: Entrepreneurs need to continually improve their skills and knowledge in order to stay ahead of the curve. This includes developing new skills and knowledge areas, such as marketing, finance, and technology.

- Developing Innovative Ideas: Continuous learning and personal growth can help entrepreneurs to develop innovative ideas and solutions to problems. By staying up-to-date with the latest trends and technologies, entrepreneurs can identify new opportunities and develop unique solutions to customer problems.

- Building a Strong Reputation: Continuous learning and personal growth can help entrepreneurs to build a strong reputation as thought leaders and experts in their field. This can lead to increased credibility, and attract new customers and business partners.

How to Cultivate a Mindset of Continuous Learning and Personal Growth?

Cultivating a mindset of continuous learning and personal growth requires a commitment to self-improvement, and a willingness to embrace new challenges and opportunities. Here are some strategies for cultivating this mindset:

- Set Learning Goals: Entrepreneurs should set specific learning goals that align with their business objectives. This could include attending conferences, taking courses, reading books, or networking with industry experts.

- Embrace Failure: Failure is a natural part of the learning process, and entrepreneurs should embrace it as an opportunity for growth and improvement. By learning from their mistakes, entrepreneurs can develop new skills and insights that will help them to succeed in the future.

- Seek Feedback: Entrepreneurs should seek feedback from customers, mentors, and peers in order to identify areas for improvement. This feedback can help entrepreneurs to identify blind spots and develop strategies for improvement.

- Develop a Learning Plan: Entrepreneurs should develop a structured learning plan that outlines the skills and knowledge areas they need to develop in order to achieve their business objectives. This plan should include specific milestones and timelines for achieving each goal.

- Practice Reflection: Reflection is an important part of the learning process, and entrepreneurs should take time to reflect on their experiences and identify areas for improvement. This could include journaling, meditation, or seeking feedback from peers or mentors.

Conclusion:

Continuous learning and personal growth are essential for entrepreneurs who want to succeed in today's rapidly-changing business environment. By cultivating a mindset of lifelong learning, entrepreneurs can stay ahead of the curve and adapt to changing market conditions. This chapter has explored the importance of continuous learning and personal growth, and provided strategies for cultivating this mindset. By embracing these strategies, entrepreneurs can build the skills and knowledge they need to achieve their business objectives and succeed in their entrepreneurial journey.

Summary:

- Continuous learning and personal growth are essential for entrepreneurs in today's rapidly-changing business environment.

- Entrepreneurs need to be adaptable, curious, and willing to embrace new ideas and perspectives.
- Continuous learning and personal growth are important for adapting to changing market conditions, improving skills and knowledge, developing innovative ideas, and building a strong reputation.
- Strategies for cultivating a mindset of continuous learning and personal growth include setting learning goals, embracing failure, seeking feedback, developing a learning plan, and practicing reflection.
- By embracing these strategies, entrepreneurs can build the skills and knowledge they need to achieve their business objectives and succeed in their entrepreneurial journey.